Travel Journal
Croatia

VPJournals

Contact Details

Name: _____

Email address: _____

Tel: _____

Address: _____

_____

_____

Important Medical Information

Blood type: _____

Medication: _____

CONTENTS

Hi, I hope you enjoy this journal. It is packed with cool stuff and recommendations for you trip to Croatia, and has plenty of space to record details of your trip.

Have fun in Croatia

Great Places to visit in Croatia

Dubrobnik's Walls	✓
Blue Cave (Blue Grotto), Bisevo	
Upper Town, Zangreb	
Mirogoj Cemeteray, Zangreb	
Plitvice Lakes National Park	
Mljet Islands	
Old Town Dubrovnik	
Korcula Island	
Hvar Island	
Zlatni Rat Beach, Brac	
Paklenica National Park	

Museum of Broken Relationship, Zangreb	
Telascica National Park	
Vis Island	
Pag Island	
Brac Island	
Rab Island	
Zadar Region	
Split	
Dalmatia County, Hvar	
Velebit Mountain	
Diocletian's Palace, Split	
Roman Amphitheatre, Pula	

Cool Places to visit in Croatia with Kids

Diocletian's Palace, Split	✓
Grgur Ninski, Split	
Roman Amphitheatre, Pula	
Istralandia, Istria	
Brijuni Island National Park	
Losinj Island	
The Sun Salutation and Sea of Organ of Zadar	
Plitvice Lakes National Park	
Blue World, Losinj Island	
Losing Aromatic Garden	
Buzet, Northern Istria	

Hum (Smallest town in the world)	
Poreč City	
Funtana Dino Park	
Eia Eco Art Centre	
Fazana Village	
Zaton Beach, Zadar	
Nature Park Medvednica	
Maksimir Park, Zangreb	
Baredine Cave, Porec	
Krk Island	
Velebit Mountain	
Telascica National Park	

Good Places to Eat in Croatia

Konoba Feral	✓
Konoba Astarea	
Mundoaka Street Food	
Restaurant 360°	
Konoba Nicola	
Restoran Lanterna na Dolcu	
Agava	
Trilogija	
Villa Ruza Restaurant and Lounge Bar	
Restaurant Dubrovnik	
Otto Taverna	

Wine & Cheese Bar paradox	
Konoba Marjan	
Dalmatino	
Bistro Bukarica	
Bistro Francesca	
Balbi	
Pet Bunara	
Restaurant Artatore Janja	
Konoba Na Kantunu	
Ranc Restaurant	
Duksa Pizza	
Zrno bio bistro	

Best Websites to Research Further

Do some more research on the internet to plan your trip:

croatiatraveller.com
croatia.hr
visit-croatia.co.uk
lonelyplanet.com/croatia
frankaboutcroatia.com
tourist-croatia.com
wikitravel.org/en/croatia
np-mljet.hr
split.gg
Find-croatia.com

More places I want to visit on our trip

1. _____
2. _____
3. _____
4. _____
5. _____
6. _____
7. _____
8. _____
9. _____
10. _____
11. _____
12. _____
13. _____
14. _____
15. _____

Postcard List

Name:

Address:

Name:

Address:

Name:

Address:

Name:

Address:

Name:

Address:

Name:

Address:

Name:

Address:

Name:

Address:

Name:

Address:

Name:

Address:

Name:

Address:

Name:

Address:

Name:

Address:

Name:

Address:

MAIL

Packing List

✓	This Journal
	Tickets
	Passport
	Money
	Chargers
	Batteries
	Book to read
	Camera
	Tablet
	Sun glasses
	Sun cream

	Toiletries
	Water
	Watch
	Snacks
	Umbrella
	Towel
	Guide book
	Kindle
	Jacket
	Medication
	Add more below

Croatia Facts

- The tie, pen, parachute and zeppelin were all Croatian inventions. The word pen, is named after its Croatian inventor, Josip Penkala. Up to this day, Croatian is still call pens "Penkala"

- Croatian soldiers in 17th century were the first ones to wear a tie in order to distinguish themselves from other armies

- Marco Polo was born in Croatia

- The Dalmatian dog breed originated in the region of Dalmatia, Croatia

- There are six sites in Croatia that are included in UNESCO World Heritage Sites list

- One of the most brilliant scientists in the world who invented alternating current electricity is Croatian. He is Nicola Tesla

- Croatian limestone was used to construct Diocletian's Palace more than 1600 years ago. This is the same material used to construct some parts of the White House in Washington DC

- The town of Zadar's newest feature, the Sea Organ, is an unusual instrument powered by the wind and the sea and played when sea pushes air through its whistles. This organ has a series of melancholy chords and produces sound through the perforated stone stairs. It is worth visiting if you are in the area

- Croatia has a population of around 4.4 million people, just a quarter of the population of New York. It had the greatest emigration in the world after Ireland. It is a small country with a total size of 56,542 square kilometers

- Croatia still use Latin as their official script.

- The town of Hum in the Istrian peninsula of Croatia claims to be the world's smallest town with only around 20 inhabitants

- Brijuni National Park is an island that used to be the summer residence of President Tito of Yugoslavia

- Croatia has a very high quality of drinking water. It is located in Adriatic sea which is the cleanest part of Mediterranean. A recent study by Harvard University ranked Croatia as the 6th cleanest country in the world

- Croatia is a relatively new independent country, having achieved its independence from Yugoslavia on 8th October 1991

- The capital city of Croatia, Zagreb, was founded more than 900 years ago

Clothes & Shoe Sizes

Children's Shoe Sizes

UK	EUROPE	US	Japan
4	20	4½ or 5	12 ½
4 ½	21	5 or 5½	13
5	21 or 22	5½ or 6	13 ½
5 ½	22	6	13½ or 14
6	23	6½ or 7	14 or 14½
6 ½	23 or 24	7 ½	14½ or 15
7	24	7½ or 8	15
7 ½	25	8 or 9	15 ½
8	25 or 26	8½ or 9	16
8 ½	26	9½	16 ½
9	27	9½ or 10	16 ½ or 17
10	28	10½ or 11	17 ½
10½ or 11	29	11½ or 12	18
11 ½	30	12½	18 or 18 ½
12	31	13	19 or 19 ½
12 ½	31	13 or 13½	19 ½ or 20
13	32	1	20
13 ½	32 ½	1 ½	20 ½
1	33	1½ or 2	21
2	34	2½ or 3	22

Children's Clothing Sizes

UK	EUROPE	US	Australia
12m	80cm	12-18m	12m
18m	80-86cm	18-24m	18m
24m	86-92cm	23-24m	2
2-3	92-98cm	2T	3
3-4	98-104cm	4T	4
3-5	104-110cm	5	5
5-6	110-116cm	6	6
6-7	116-122cm	6X-7	7
7-8	122-128cm	7 to 8	8
8-9	128-134cm	9 to 10	9
9-10	134-140cm	10	10
10-11	140-146cm	11	11
11-12	146-152cm	14	12

Women's Shoe Sizes

UK	EUROPE	US	Japan
3	35 ½	5	22 ½
3 ½	36	5 ½	23
4	37	6	23
4 ½	37 ½	6 ½	23 ½
5	38	7	24
5 ½	39	7 ½	24
6	39 ½	8	24 ½
6 ½	40	8 ½	25
7	41	9 ½	25 ½
7 ½	41 ½	10	26
8	42	10 ½	26 ½

Women's Clothes Sizes

UK	US	Japan	France / Spain	Germany	Croatia	Australia
6/8	6	7-9	36	34	40	8
10	8	9-11	38	36	42	10
12	10	11-13	40	38	44	12
14	12	13-15	42	39	46	14
16	14	15-17	44	40	48	16
18	16	17-19	46	42	50	18
20	18	19-21	48	44	52	20

Men's Shoe Sizes

UK	EUROPE	US	Japan
6	38 ½	6 ½	24 ½
6 ½	39	7	25
7	40	7 ½	25 ½
7 ½	41	8	26
8	42	8 ½	27 ½
8 ½	43	9	27 ½
9	43 ½	9 ½	28
9 ½	44	10	28 ½
10	44	10 ½	28 ½
10 ½	44 ½	11	29
11	45	12	29 ½

Men's Suit / Coat / Sweater Sizes

UK / US / Aus	EU / Japan	General
32	42	Small
34	44	Small
36	46	Small
38	48	Medium
40	50	Large
42	52	Large
44	54	Extra Large
46	56	Extra Large

Men's Pants / Trouser Sizes (Waist)

UK / US	Europe
32	81 cm
34	86 cm
36	91 cm
38	97 cm
40	102 cm
42	107 cm

We have included another copy of this at the back of the book, so you can find it quickly again when you are in Croatia

Croatia Trip Diary

Write a daily diary during your trip

Day 1

Date: _____   **Weather:** _____

Day 2

Date: _____   **Weather:** _____

_____

_____

_____

_____

_____

_____

_____

_____

_____

_____

_____

_____

Day 3

Date: _____   **Weather:** _____

Day 4

Date: _____   **Weather:** _____

Day 5

Date: _____   **Weather:** _____

_____

_____

_____

_____

_____

_____

_____

_____

_____

_____

_____

_____

_____

_____

Day 6

Date: _____   **Weather:** _____

Day 7

Date: _____   **Weather:** _____

Day 8

Date: _____   **Weather:** _____

Day 9

Date: _____   **Weather:** _____

Day 10

Date: _____   **Weather:** _____

Day 11

Date: _____   **Weather:** _____

_____

_____

_____

_____

_____

_____

_____

_____

_____

_____

_____

_____

_____

_____

Day 12

Date: _____   **Weather:** _____

_____

_____

_____

_____

_____

_____

_____

_____

_____

_____

_____

_____

_____

_____

Day 13

Date: _____   **Weather:** _____

Day 14

Date: _____   **Weather:** _____

_____

_____

_____

_____

_____

_____

_____

_____

_____

_____

_____

_____

_____

Day 15

Date: _____   **Weather:** _____

_____

_____

_____

_____

_____

_____

_____

_____

_____

_____

_____

_____

_____

Day 16

Date: _____   Weather: _____

_____

_____

_____

_____

_____

_____

_____

_____

_____

_____

_____

_____

_____

_____

_____

_____

_____

_____

_____

Day 17

Date: _____   **Weather:** _____

_____

_____

_____

_____

_____

_____

_____

_____

_____

_____

_____

_____

_____

_____

_____

_____

_____

_____

Day 18

Date: _____   Weather: _____

Day 19

Date: _____   **Weather:** _____

_____

_____

_____

_____

_____

_____

_____

_____

_____

_____

_____

_____

_____

_____

_____

_____

Day 20

Date: _____　　**Weather:** _____

_____

_____

_____

_____

_____

_____

_____

_____

_____

_____

_____

_____

_____

_____

Day 21

Date: _____   **Weather:** _____

Memories of your Trip

Things I will remember from the trip

Favorite Places visited on the Trip

People I Met

Name:
Address:
Tel:
email:

Name:
Address:
Tel:
email:

Name:
Address:
Tel:
email:

Name:
Address:
Tel:
email:

Name:
Address:
Tel:
email:

Name:
Address:
Tel:
email:

Name:
Address:
Tel:
email:

Name:	
Address:	
Tel:	
email:	

Name:	
Address:	
Tel:	
email:	

Name:	
Address:	
Tel:	
email:	

Name:	
Address:	
Tel:	
email:	

We hope you enjoyed your trip to Croatia

Please leave us a review if you found this Journal useful

Check out our useful resources on the next few pages

Clothes & Shoe Sizes

Children's Shoe Sizes

UK	EUROPE	US	Japan
4	20	4½ or 5	12 ½
4 ½	21	5 or 5½	13
5	21 or 22	5½ or 6	13 ½
5 ½	22	6	13½ or 14
6	23	6½ or 7	14 or 14½
6 ½	23 or 24	7 ½	14½ or 15
7	24	7½ or 8	15
7 ½	25	8 or 9	15 ½
8	25 or 26	8½ or 9	16
8 ½	26	9½	16 ½
9	27	9½ or 10	16 ½ or 17
10	28	10½ or 11	17 ½
10½ or 11	29	11½ or 12	18
11 ½	30	12½	18 or 18 ½
12	31	13	19 or 19 ½
12 ½	31	13 or 13½	19 ½ or 20
13	32	1	20
13 ½	32 ½	1 ½	20 ½
1	33	1½ or 2	21
2	34	2½ or 3	22

Children's Clothing Sizes

UK	EUROPE	US	Australia
12m	80cm	12-18m	12m
18m	80-86cm	18-24m	18m
24m	86-92cm	23-24m	2
2-3	92-98cm	2T	3
3-4	98-104cm	4T	4
3-5	104-110cm	5	5
5-6	110-116cm	6	6
6-7	116-122cm	6X-7	7
7-8	122-128cm	7 to 8	8
8-9	128-134cm	9 to 10	9
9-10	134-140cm	10	10
10-11	140-146cm	11	11
11-12	146-152cm	14	12

Women's Shoe Sizes

UK	EUROPE	US	Japan
3	35 ½	5	22 ½
3 ½	36	5 ½	23
4	37	6	23
4 ½	37 ½	6 ½	23 ½
5	38	7	24
5 ½	39	7 ½	24
6	39 ½	8	24 ½
6 ½	40	8 ½	25
7	41	9 ½	25 ½
7 ½	41 ½	10	26
8	42	10 ½	26 ½

Women's Clothes Sizes

UK	US	Japan	France / Spain	Germany	Croatia	Australia
6/8	6	7-9	36	34	40	8
10	8	9-11	38	36	42	10
12	10	11-13	40	38	44	12
14	12	13-15	42	39	46	14
16	14	15-17	44	40	48	16
18	16	17-19	46	42	50	18
20	18	19-21	48	44	52	20

Men's Shoe Sizes

UK	EUROPE	US	Japan
6	38 ½	6 ½	24 ½
6 ½	39	7	25
7	40	7 ½	25 ½
7 ½	41	8	26
8	42	8 ½	27 ½
8 ½	43	9	27 ½
9	43 ½	9 ½	28
9 ½	44	10	28 ½
10	44	10 ½	28 ½
10 ½	44 ½	11	29
11	45	12	29 ½

Men's Suit / Coat / Sweater Sizes

UK / US / Aus	EU / Japan	General
32	42	Small
34	44	Small
36	46	Small
38	48	Medium
40	50	Large
42	52	Large
44	54	Extra Large
46	56	Extra Large

Men's Pants / Trouser Sizes (Waist)

UK / US	Europe
32	81 cm
34	86 cm
36	91 cm
38	97 cm
40	102 cm
42	107 cm

Common Translations

English	French	Spanish	Croatian
Hello	Bonjour	Hola	**Zdravo**
Goodbye	Au revoir	Adiós	**Dovidenja**
Yes	Oui	Sí	**Da**
No	Non	No	**Ne**
Please	S'il-vous-plaît	Por favor	**Molim**
Thank you	Merci	Gracias	**Hvala ti**
Excuse me	Excusez-moi	Perdón	**Ispricajte me**
How much	Combien	Cuánto	**Koliko**
My name is	Mon nom est	Mi nombre es	**Moje ime je**
Where is	Où est	Dónde está	**Gdje je**
The bank	La banque	El banco	**Banka**
The toilet	Les toilettes	El baño	**Toalet**

German	Japanese	Mandarin	Italian
Hallo	Kon'nichiwa	Ni hao	Ciao
Auf Wiedersehen	Sayonara	Zaijian	Arrivederci
Ja	Hai	Shi de	Si
Nein	Ie	Meiyou	No
Bitte	Onegaishimasu	Qing	Per favore
Vielen Dank	Arigato	Xiexie	Grazie
Entschuldigung	Sumimasen	Duoshao	Mi scusi
Wie viel	Ikura	Wo de mingzi shi	Quanto
Mein Name ist	Watashinonamaeha	Nali	Io mi chiamo
Wo ist	Doko ni aru	Yinhang	Dov'è
Die Bank	Ginko	Yinhang	La banca
Die Toilette	Toire	Cesuo	Il bagno

Notes: